Origami

The art & fun of Japanese paper folding

MAKIKO IKEDA

Additional Material by
JENNIFER LANG

MUD PUDDLE BOOKS, INC.
New York, New York

Origami:
The art & fun of Japanese paper folding

ISBN: 1-59412-106-0

This edition published 2005 by
Mud Puddle Books, Inc.
54 W. 21st Street
Suite 601
New York, NY 10010
info@mudpuddlebooks.com

Material originally published by
Hinkler Books Pty Ltd.,
17-23 Redwood Drive
Dingley, Victoria, 3172, Australia

Special contents of this edition
© 2005 by Hinkler Books Pty Ltd.

Original Hinkler editions:
Origami by Makiko Ikeda
© 2001 by Hinkler Books Pty Ltd.

Origami Monsters by Jennifer Lang
© 2005 by Hinkler Books Pty Ltd.

Printed in China

Contents

Introduction

Origami is a Japanese word, which means 'paper folding'. It was first practiced almost a thousand years ago at the Imperial Court, where it was considered an amusing and elegant way of passing the time. Over the centuries the skill was passed on to the ordinary people, who took it up with enthusiasm and made it into a folk art.

Origami is still used in Japan as a teaching and learning tool, and this charming and inexpensive activity has now become immensely popular worldwide.

There are so many things you can make with origami, by folding a simple square of paper into various different shapes. In this book, you will be introduced to a number of traditional origami designs which have been passed down through the generations in Japanese families.

Needless to say, the 'folding' itself is fun, but it is even more enjoyable to make use of the finished creations in various ways. They can be used as functional items, unique gifts, decorations or charming toys.

Some ideas on how to use your finished origami are included in the book, but we hope you will think of many other creative uses for them.

Makiko & Shun Ikeda

Tips

Even though origami is as easy as simply folding a piece of paper, here are a few guidelines to help make the process more enjoyable and satisfying.

✓ Choose the paper you use for origami carefully. Obviously color plays an important part in the success of many of the projects. You can buy special origami paper from art and craft stores, or you can try using different kinds of paper, including gift wrap, which you can find at home. When using non-specialty paper for your origami work, you need to make sure that it will fold and crease well.

✓ Check that your paper is exactly square. If it isn't, you will need to trim it with scissors or a sharp knife. A sharp knife will need adult supervision.

✓ When making folds, it helps to look ahead to the next step to see how the fold will look after it has been made.

✓ Make your creases on a firm, flat surface, not for instance on a carpet or tablecloth. Precise folds and creases are the secret to successful origami designs. When you are sure you have folded the paper in the right place, run your fingernail across the fold to make it crisp and neat.

Symbols & Folding Techniques

★   1 star - easy to make

★★   2 stars - more advanced

★★★   3 stars - for the experts!

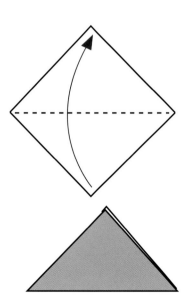

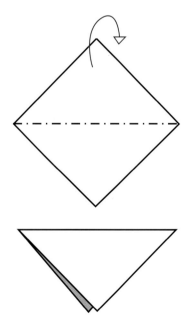

Valley Fold

Fold forward in the direction of the arrow, so that the crease is at the bottom of two sides of paper, like a valley.

Mountain Fold

Fold to the reverse side in the direction of the arrow, so that the crease is at the top of two sides of paper, like a mountain fold.

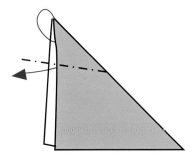

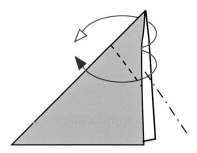

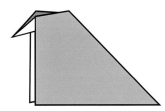

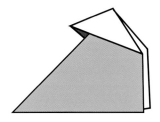

Inside Fold

Fold the paper forward and backward to make a crease. Open out and push the point down inside along the creases you have just made, then fold together again so that the point juts out.

Cover Fold

Fold the paper forward and backward to make a crease. Open out and fold point up and back along the creases you have just made, then fold together again to form a cover.

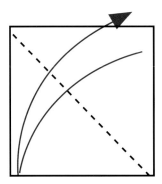

Make a Crease

Fold the paper as shown in the diagram, and then open it out again.

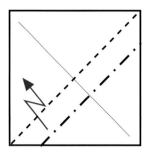

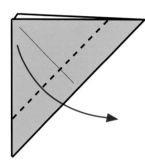

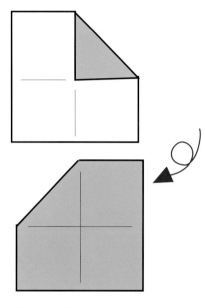

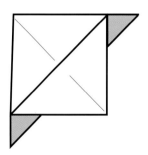

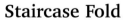

Staircase Fold

This fold needs to look like a series of steps when it's seen from the side.

Turn Over

When you see this symbol, turn the paper over.

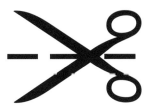

Cut

Cut along the line as shown.

Blow Up

Gently blow air in the direction
shown by the arrow..

Press, Press Down

Gently press in the direction
shown by the arrow.

Easy Animal Faces

Making these charming animal faces is a good way to practice the creases and folds before moving on to more complex projects. They can be used to make unique greeting cards, or by adding an ice cream stick you can turn them into puppets. Try adding a cotton thread and hanging them on the Christmas tree.

Cow's Face ★

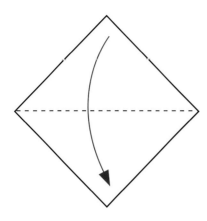

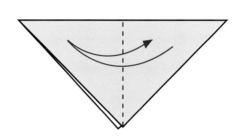

1. Fold the paper in half into a triangle.

2. Fold in half again along the dotted line as shown on the diagram, to make creases. Open out.

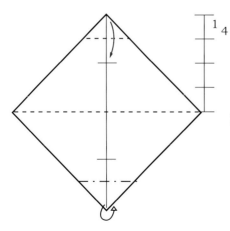

1_4

3. Now fold down the top corner a quarter of the way to the middle and fold up the bottom corner a quarter of the way to the middle on the reverse side.

4. Fold down at the middle.

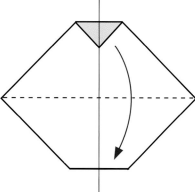

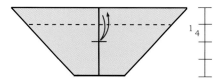

5. Fold down along the dotted line. Unfold.

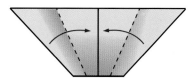

6. Fold the edges to the center crease.

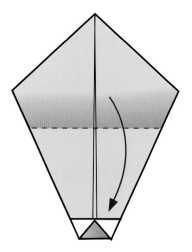

7. Now you need to fold the top corners down on the crease made in step 5. (As you can't see that crease from the front where you're working, you'll need to look at the back of the paper to remind yourself where it is.)

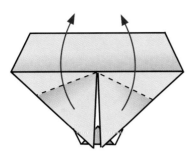

8. Fold both the bottom corners up diagonally. Turn over.

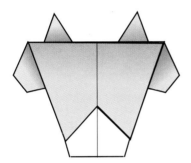

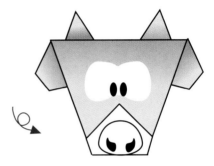

9. To finish your cow's face, draw on big round eyes and a nose.

Elephant's Face ★

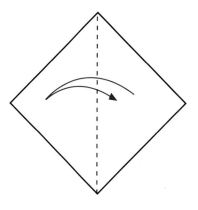

1. First fold the paper into a triangle and make a crease. Unfold.

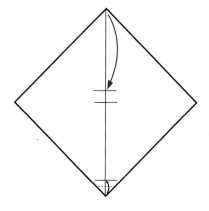

2. Fold down the top corner to the point slightly above center and fold up the bottom corner just a little. See the diagram for scale of folds.

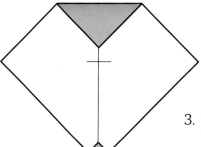

3. This is what it will look like. Turn over the paper.

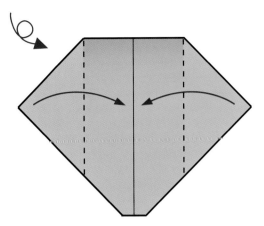

4. Fold both sides in along the dotted lines.

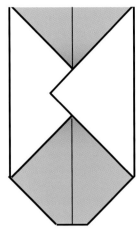

5. This is how it should look now. Turn over.

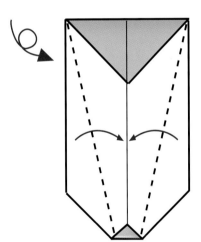

6. Fold both edges in again along the dotted lines.

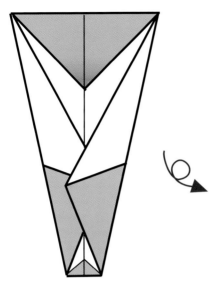

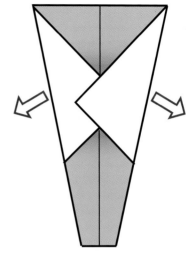

7. It should now look like this.
   Turn over again.

8. Unfold the two flaps
   facing you.

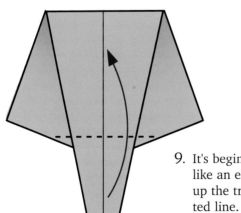

9. It's beginning to look a little
   like an elephant's face! Fold
   up the trunk along the dotted line.

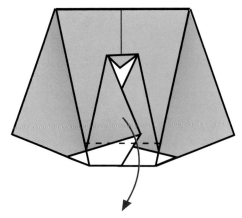

10. Fold the trunk down again as shown, so the tusks appear.

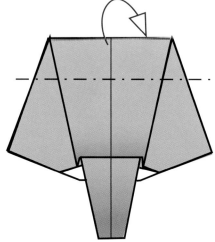

11. Fold the top edge back (mountain fold) along the dotted line.

12. Now all you need to do is draw on an elephant's face.

Dog and Cat Faces

Dog and Cat faces both start with the same two folds.

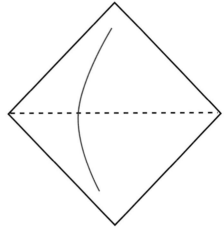

1. First fold paper into a triangle.

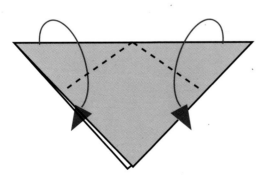

2. Fold corners down diagonally.

To complete the dog:

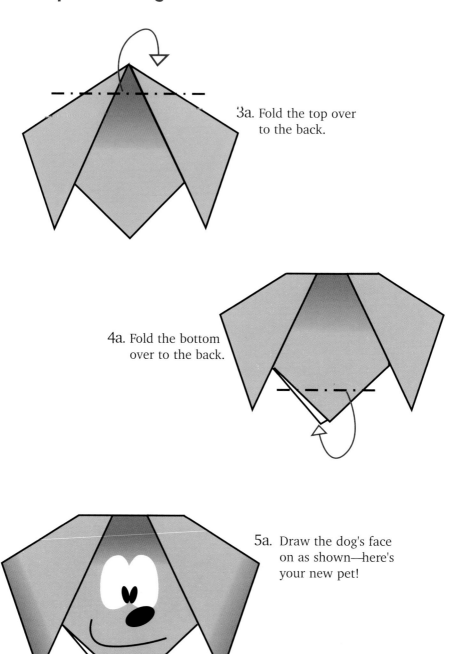

3a. Fold the top over to the back.

4a. Fold the bottom over to the back.

5a. Draw the dog's face on as shown—here's your new pet!

To complete the cat:

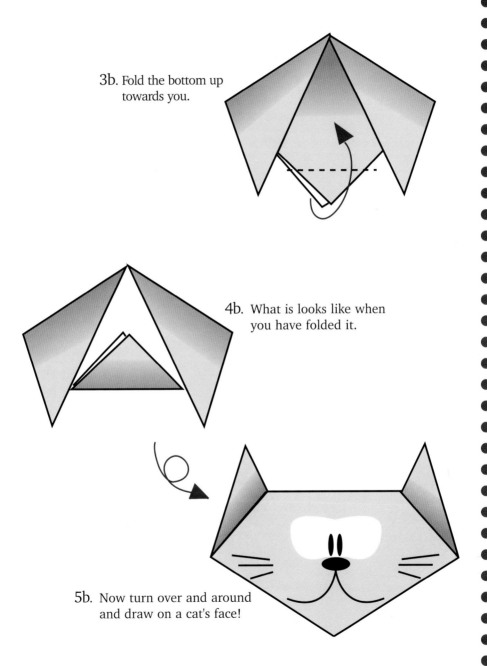

3b. Fold the bottom up towards you.

4b. What is looks like when you have folded it.

5b. Now turn over and around and draw on a cat's face!

All Things Bright and Beautiful

The projects in this section are fun to make and gradually becoming more challenging. Make a paper cup that really holds water, a whole street full of houses, or a beautiful star-shaped container.

Balloon ★★

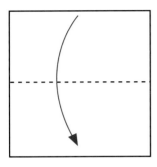

1. First fold the paper in half.

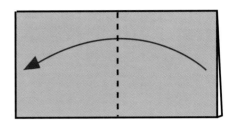

2. Fold in half again, right to left.

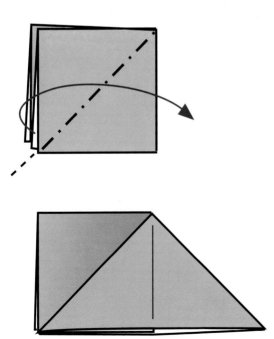

3, 4 and 5.
Spread out the top flap from the inside and fold by pressing down so that it looks like the diagram in step 5. Turn over.

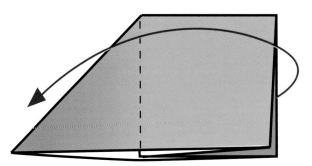

6. Swing the right hand edge to the left

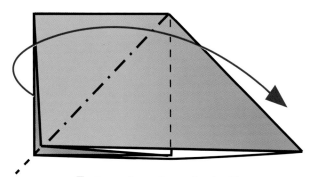

7. Spread out from the inside and fold by pressing down.

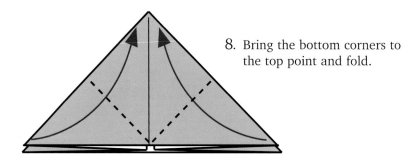

8. Bring the bottom corners to the top point and fold.

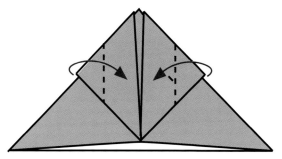

9. Bring the side corners to the center and fold as shown.

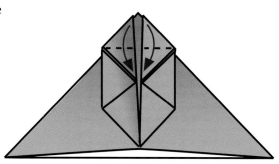

10. Fold top corners down.

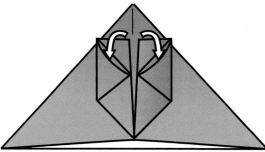

11. Fold the corners over again and tuck corners into the pockets. Turn over.

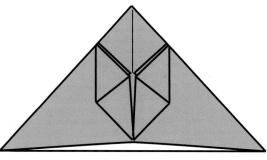

12. Repeat steps 8 to 11 on the other side.

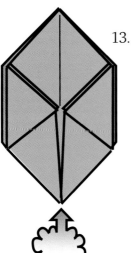

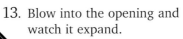

13. Blow into the opening and
    watch it expand.

14. Here it is finished.

Pencil ★★

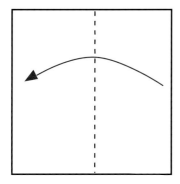

1. First, fold the paper in half.

2. Fold down the top flap edge A to meet edge B and fold along the dotted line.

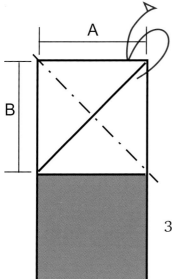

3. Make a mountain fold so that edge A is aligned with edge B on the other side. Open out again.

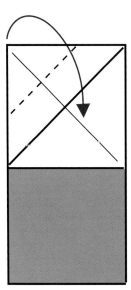

4. Now fold down the corner along the dotted line so it juts out a little from the center.

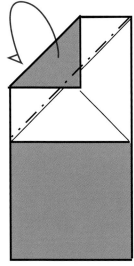

5. Make a mountain fold at the crease to the reverse side.

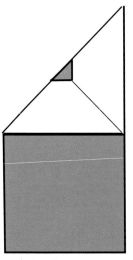

6. This is what your pencil model should look like now. Turn over.

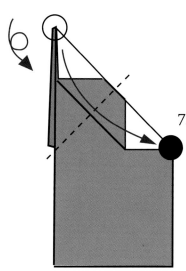

7. Bring the top corner down in a valley fold along the dotted line and fold carefully so the top point (white circle) meets the point on the right (black circle).

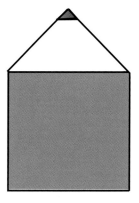

8. You've made a thick pencil.

To make a thin pencil:

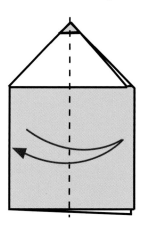

9. Make a valley fold in your thick pencil as shown to make a crease. Unfold.

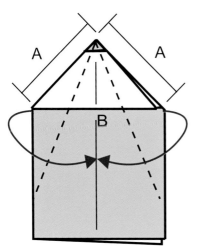

10. Now fold both outer edges (A) into the center line (B) and press gently.

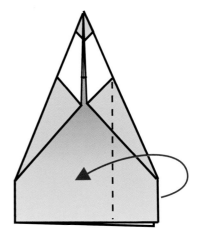

11. Fold the right flap in along the dotted line as shown.

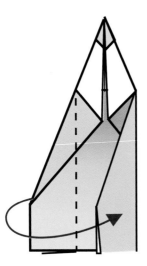

12. Fold the other side in to match.

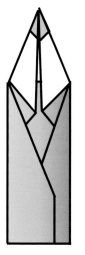

13. This is what the folded model should look like now. Turn over.

14. And you now have a thin pencil.

Bookmark

Punch a hole at the end and tie a ribbon through it to create a charming bookmark.

You could make a set of colored pencils by using a different colored sheet for each pencil you make.

Star-Shaped Box ★★

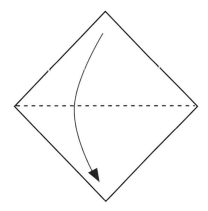

1. First, fold the paper in half into a triangle shape.

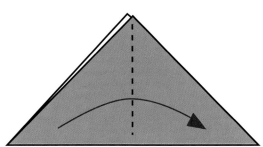

2. Fold in half again, along the dotted line.

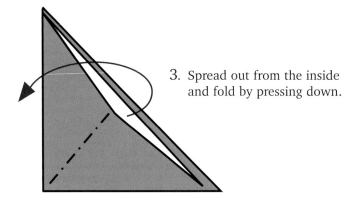

3. Spread out from the inside and fold by pressing down.

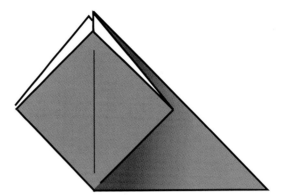

4. This is what it should look like. Turn over.

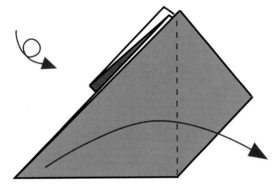

5. Swing the point over to the opposite side.

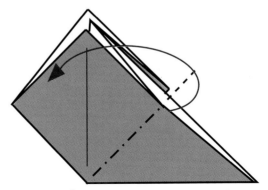

6. Spread out from the inside and fold by pressing down.

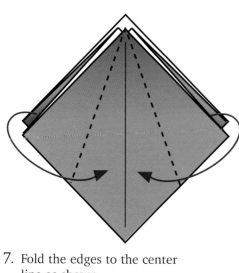

7. Fold the edges to the center line as shown.

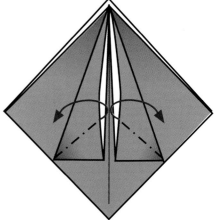

8. Open the sides by sliding your fingers inside, and flatten.

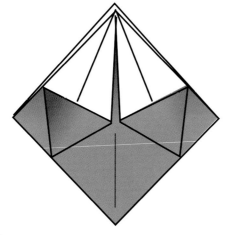

9. Turn over and do the same for the other side.

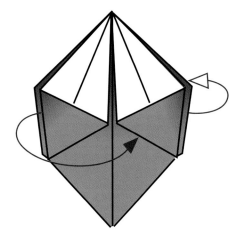

10. Fold the top left layer to the right. Turn over and repeat.

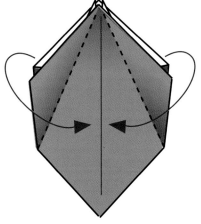

11. Fold edges of the top layer to the center line.

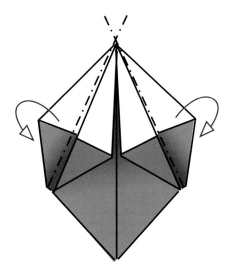

12. Fold other edges (in mountain folds) to the back along the lines.

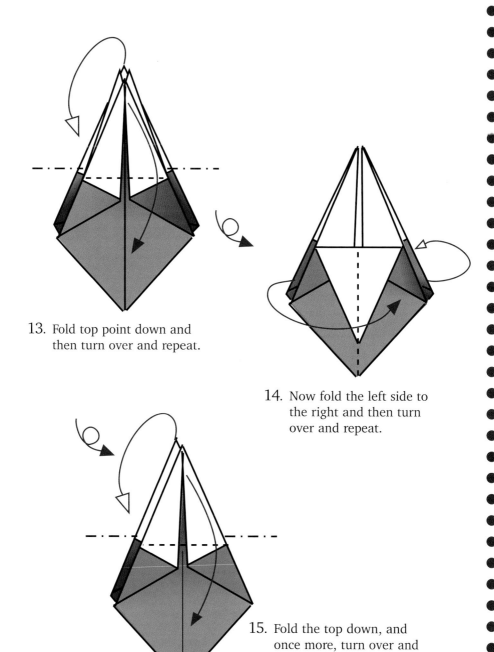

13. Fold top point down and then turn over and repeat.

14. Now fold the left side to the right and then turn over and repeat.

15. Fold the top down, and once more, turn over and repeat.

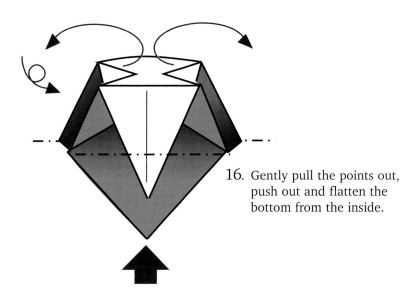

16. Gently pull the points out,
    push out and flatten the
    bottom from the inside.

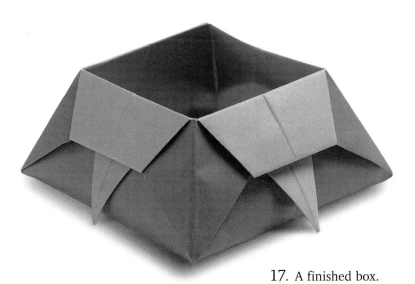

17. A finished box.

Paper Cup ★

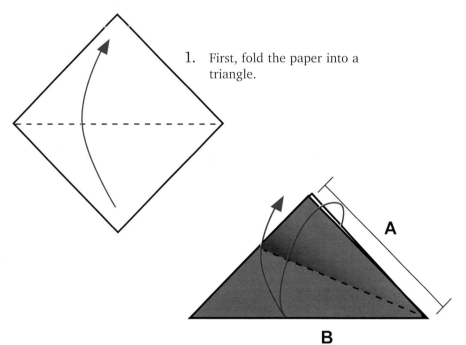

1. First, fold the paper into a triangle.

2. Align one edge of A with edge B and make a crease.

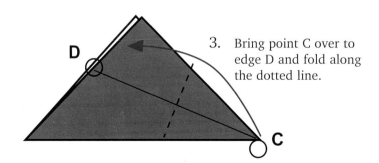

3. Bring point C over to edge D and fold along the dotted line.

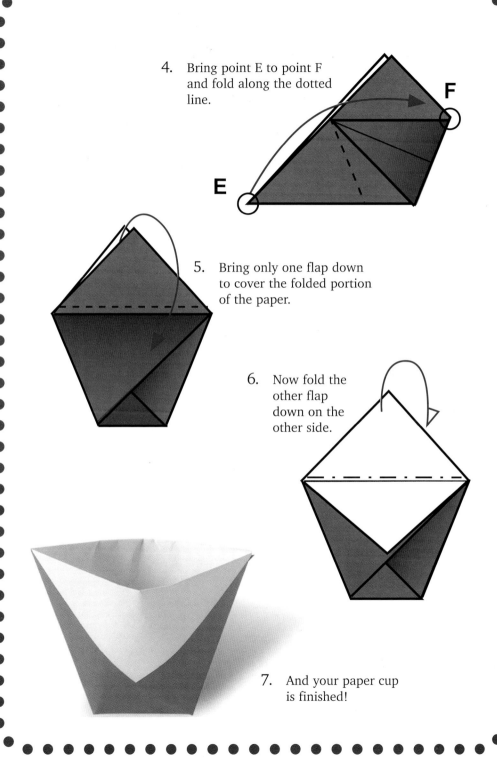

4. Bring point E to point F and fold along the dotted line.

F

E

5. Bring only one flap down to cover the folded portion of the paper.

6. Now fold the other flap down on the other side.

7. And your paper cup is finished!

39

Top ★★

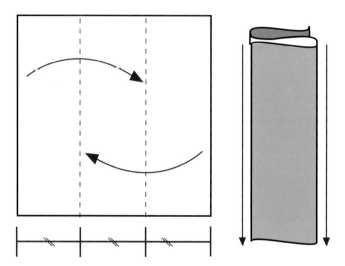

1. Take one of the squares of paper and fold it into thirds. If you first crease it lightly into three equal portions, it is easier to fold.

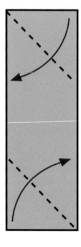

2. Fold the two opposite corners into triangles.

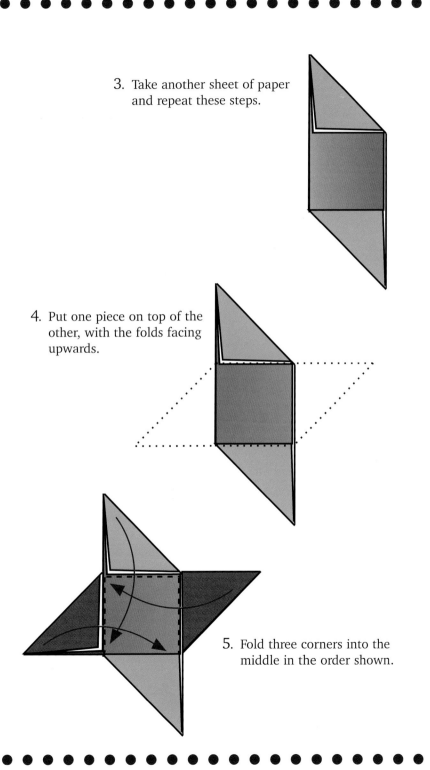

3. Take another sheet of paper and repeat these steps.

4. Put one piece on top of the other, with the folds facing upwards.

5. Fold three corners into the middle in the order shown.

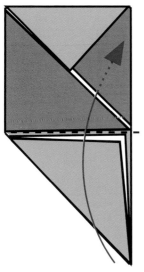

6. Tuck the last corner inside.

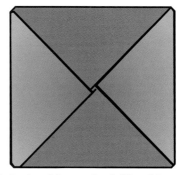

7. It should now look like this.

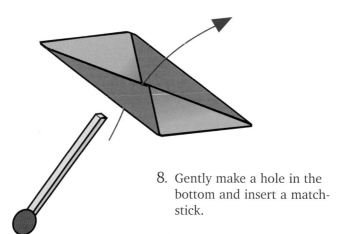

8. Gently make a hole in the bottom and insert a match-stick.

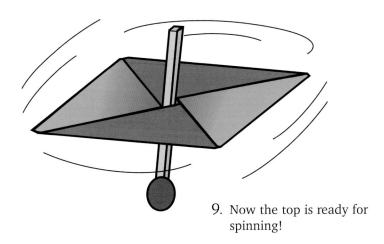

9. Now the top is ready for
   spinning!

House ★

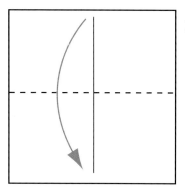

1. Crease paper in half and unfold. Then fold side edges together.

2. Fold the right and left edges of the paper towards the center.

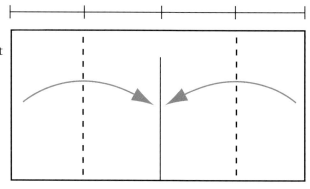

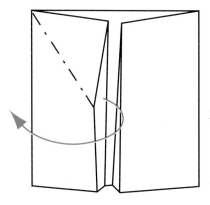

3. Pull the two upper corners outwards and flatten them, then repeat on the other side.

4. Turn your creation over. If you like,
you can give your house a name.

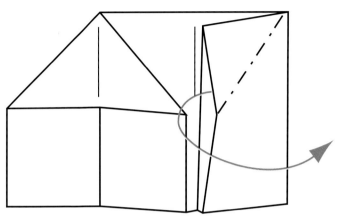

SHADY TREE
MANOR

All Creatures Great and Small

This section is devoted to birds, fish, animals and even an insect. There is also an extinct animal—the dinosaur. It is interesting and fun to make each of the designs, but you can use your imagination and go further. Try making several pigeons and hanging them on a mobile, or make lots of dinosaurs in different colors and sizes and create a theme park. Or perhaps you could make an aquarium using a box and some cellophane, and fill it with goldfish, turtles and whales . . .

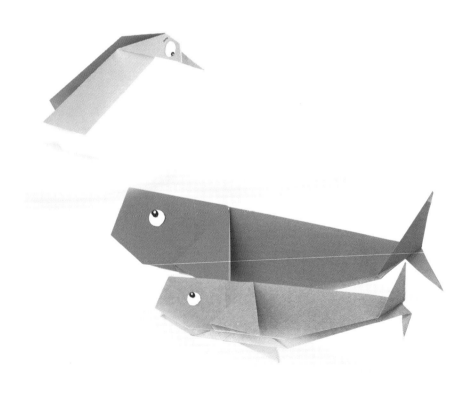

Whale ★★

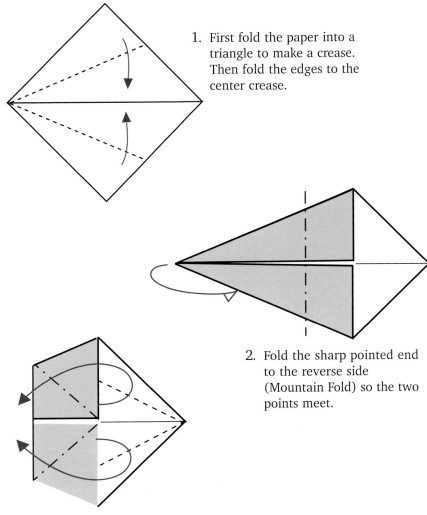

1. First fold the paper into a triangle to make a crease. Then fold the edges to the center crease.

2. Fold the sharp pointed end to the reverse side (Mountain Fold) so the two points meet.

3. Open both flaps from the inside and fold by pressing down firmly.

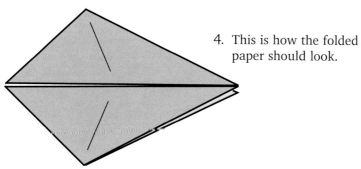

4. This is how the folded
   paper should look.

5. Fold the top flat to the left
   along the dotted line.

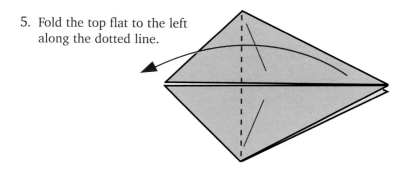

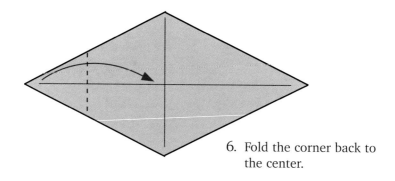

6. Fold the corner back to
   the center.

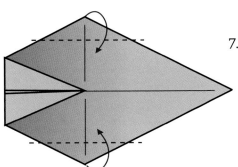

7. Now fold both edge corners horizontally along the dotted lines.

8. Fold all layers horizontally along the center.

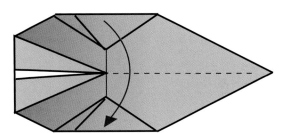

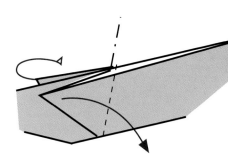

9. Then fold the corner down diagonally. Do the same on the other side.

10. Spread out from the underside and fold over the portion of the tail to form a Cover Fold.

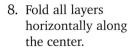

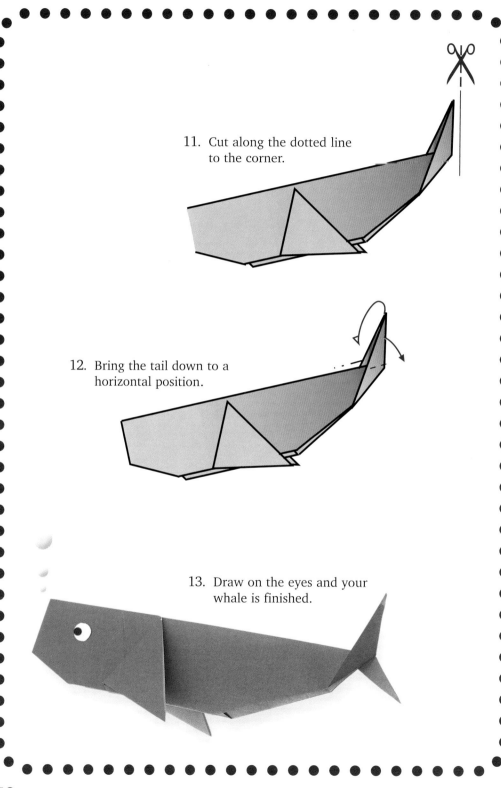

11. Cut along the dotted line to the corner.

12. Bring the tail down to a horizontal position.

13. Draw on the eyes and your whale is finished.

Penguin ★★

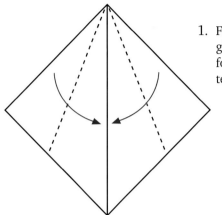

1. Fold the paper into a triangle and make a crease. Then fold the edges in to the center crease.

2. Fold in half away from you (Mountain Fold) along the center crease.

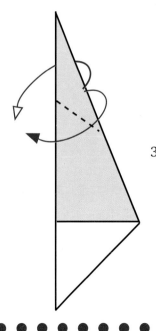

3. Fold back and forth along the dotted line to make a deep crease. Open out the sheet of paper and push the tip down, and at the same time close up the paper again, so the tip folds over as shown (Cover Fold).

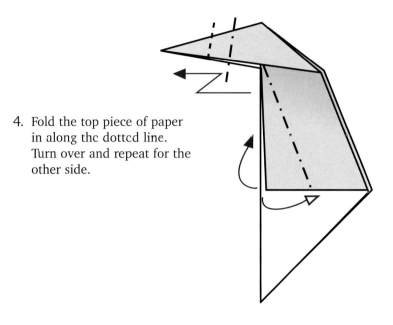

4. Fold the top piece of paper
   in along the dotted line.
   Turn over and repeat for the
   other side.

5. Turn over and fold the head
   into a Staircase Fold.

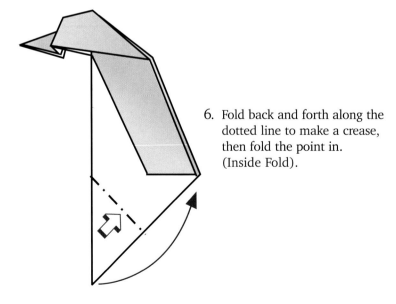

6. Fold back and forth along the
   dotted line to make a crease,
   then fold the point in.
   (Inside Fold).

7. Fold the bottom tips in as shown in the diagram.

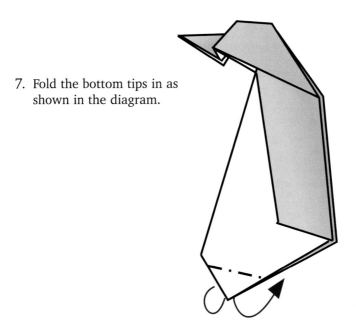

8. Draw an eye in carefully—and your penguin is finished.

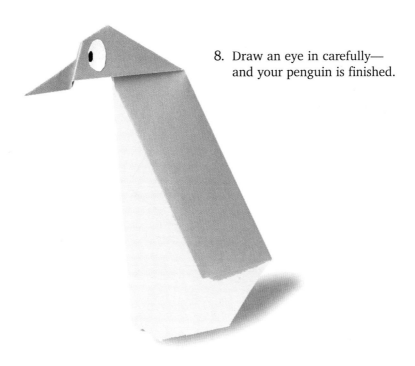

Pig ★★

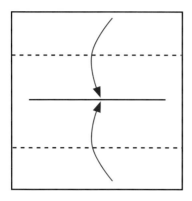

1. First fold the paper in half to make a crease. Now bring the bottom and top edges to the center crease and fold.

2. Fold all corners into the center line to make creases. Unfold all.

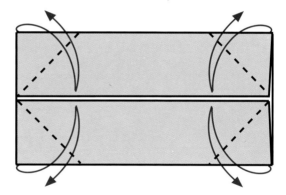

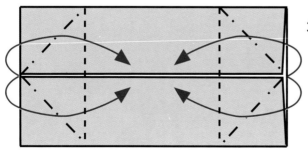

3. Make vertical valley folds where indicated, then using the diagram as a guide, pull corners out and fold down.

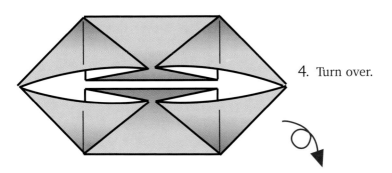

4. Turn over.

5. Fold in half.

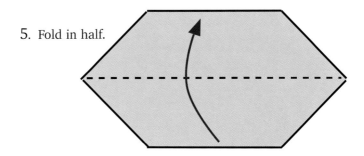

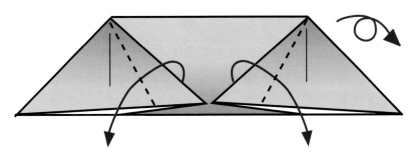

6. Now fold the inside flaps along the dotted lines diagonally so the corners all point down. Turn over and repeat.

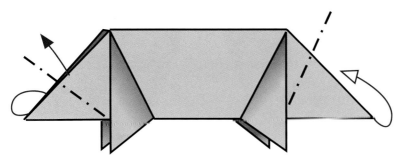

7. Fold the point at one end up inside to make a nose, and then fold the point at the other end inside to make its bottom.

8. Draw in some eyes and your pig is finished!

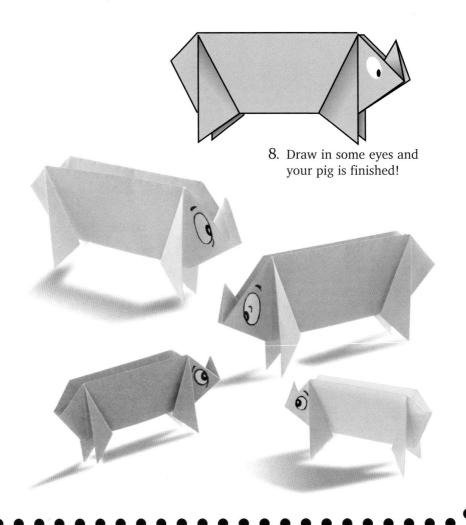

Flying Crane ★★

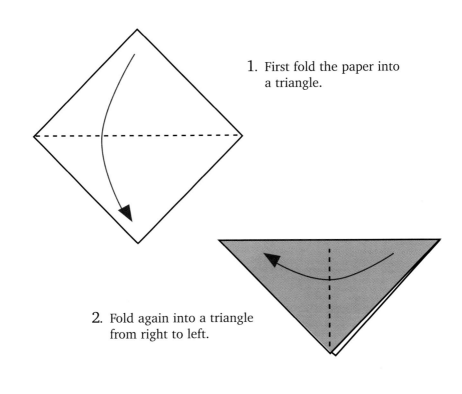

1. First fold the paper into a triangle.

2. Fold again into a triangle from right to left.

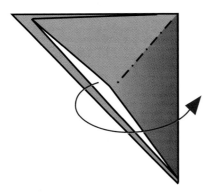

3. Spread out from the inside and fold by pressing down gently on the layers.

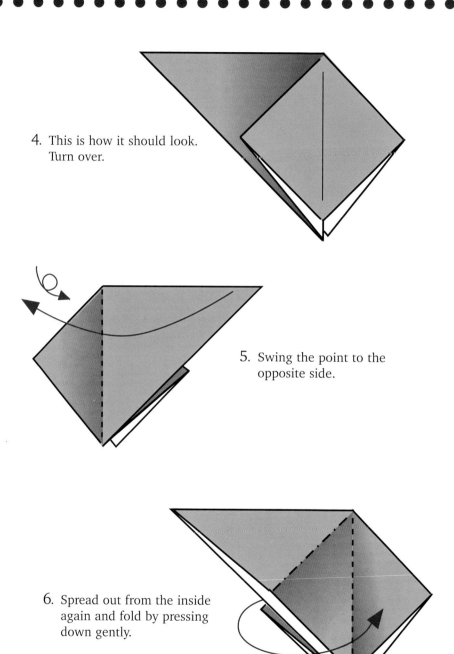

4. This is how it should look. Turn over.

5. Swing the point to the opposite side.

6. Spread out from the inside again and fold by pressing down gently.

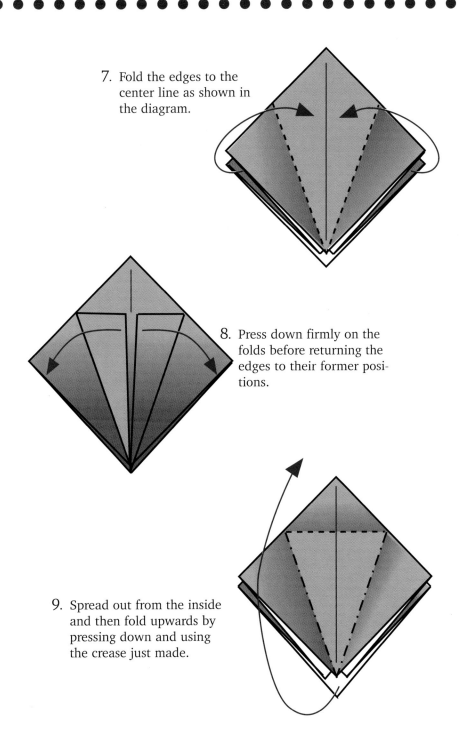

7. Fold the edges to the center line as shown in the diagram.

8. Press down firmly on the folds before returning the edges to their former positions.

9. Spread out from the inside and then fold upwards by pressing down and using the crease just made.

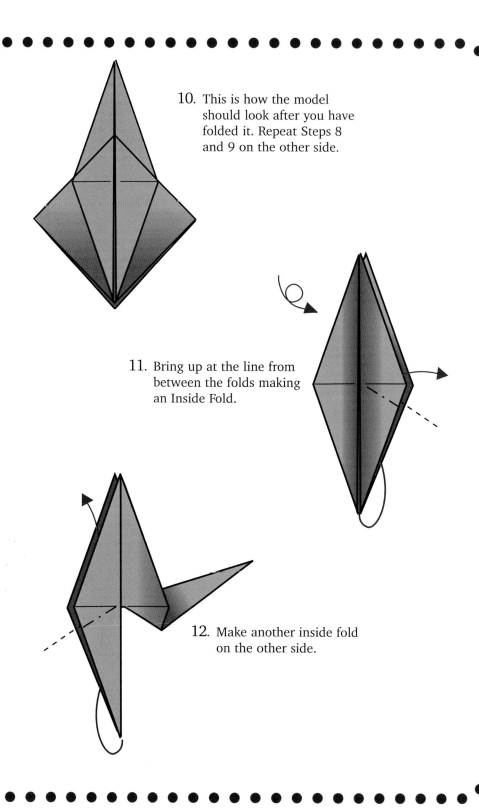

10. This is how the model should look after you have folded it. Repeat Steps 8 and 9 on the other side.

11. Bring up at the line from between the folds making an Inside Fold.

12. Make another inside fold on the other side.

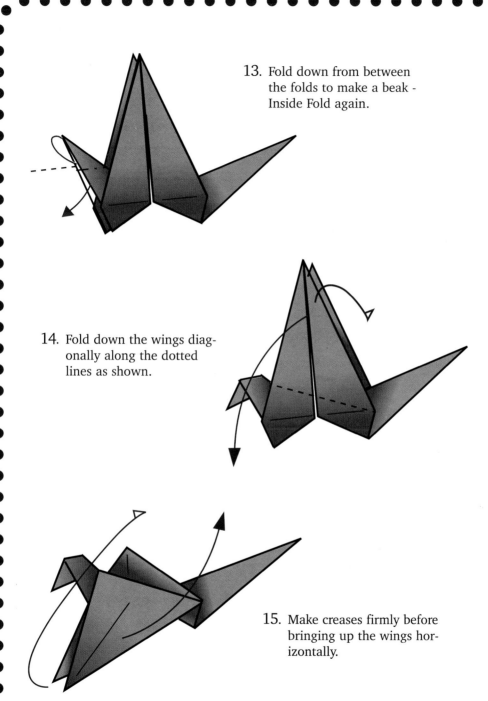

13. Fold down from between
    the folds to make a beak -
    Inside Fold again.

14. Fold down the wings diag-
    onally along the dotted
    lines as shown.

15. Make creases firmly before
    bringing up the wings hor-
    izontally.

You can make your crane appear to fly by holding it with one hand as shown, and pulling the tail gently with the other to make the wings flap.

Pigeon ★★

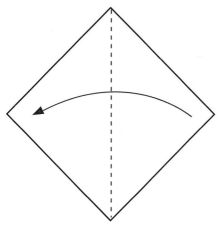

1. First fold the paper into a triangle.

2. Fold both corners along the dotted line seen in the diagram to the side so the corners stick out.

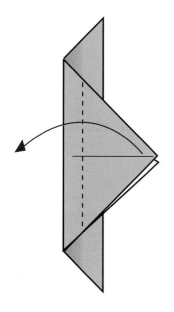

3. Now fold just the flap facing you to the side along the dotted line on the diagram so it sticks out on the other side.

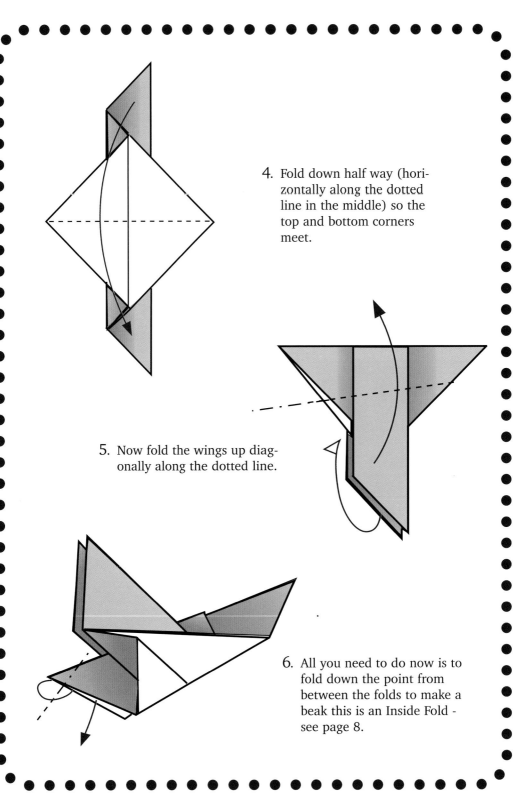

4. Fold down half way (horizontally along the dotted line in the middle) so the top and bottom corners meet.

5. Now fold the wings up diagonally along the dotted line.

6. All you need to do now is to fold down the point from between the folds to make a beak this is an Inside Fold - see page 8.

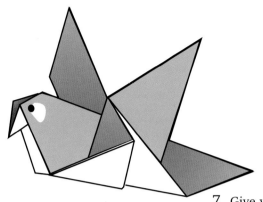

7. Give your bird some eyes and it's finished.

Goldfish ★★★

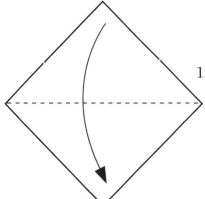

1. First fold the paper into a triangle.

2. Fold the corners down so they come together at the bottom point.

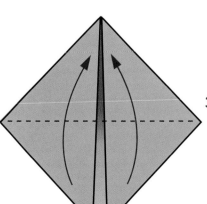

3. Now fold the bottom flaps up to the top point.

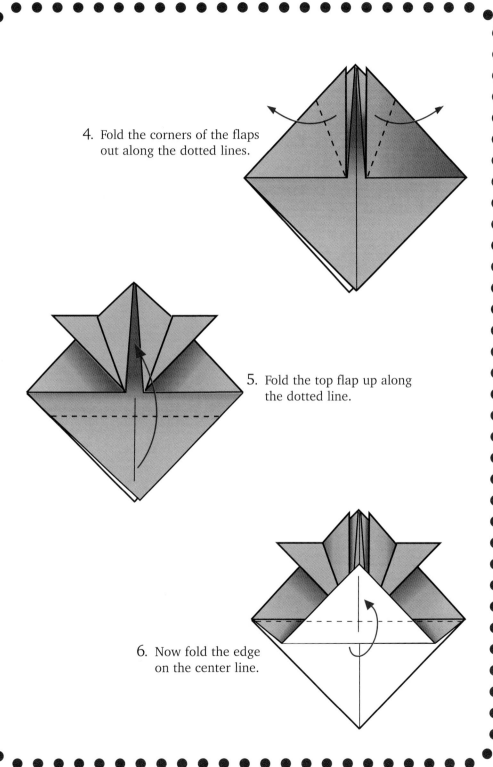

4. Fold the corners of the flaps out along the dotted lines.

5. Fold the top flap up along the dotted line.

6. Now fold the edge on the center line.

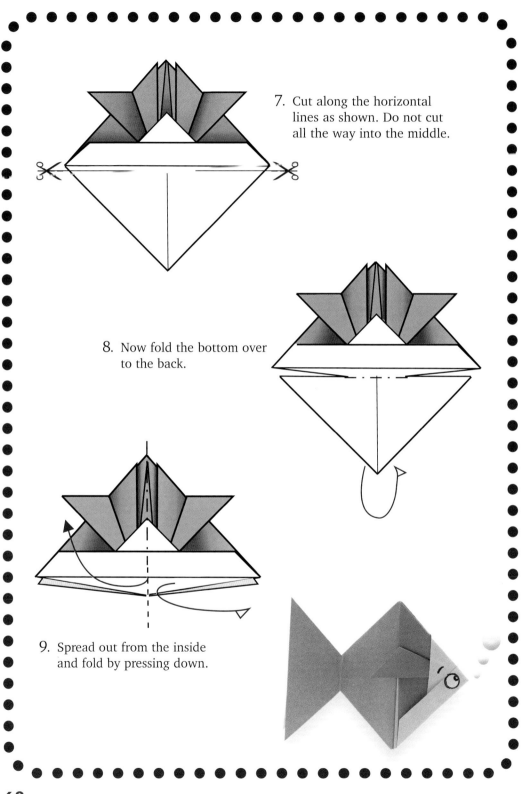

7. Cut along the horizontal lines as shown. Do not cut all the way into the middle.

8. Now fold the bottom over to the back.

9. Spread out from the inside and fold by pressing down.

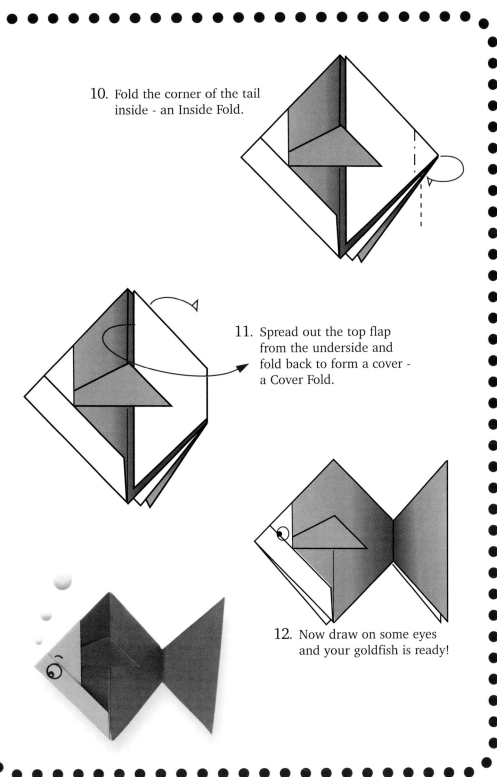

10. Fold the corner of the tail inside - an Inside Fold.

11. Spread out the top flap from the underside and fold back to form a cover - a Cover Fold.

12. Now draw on some eyes and your goldfish is ready!

Dinosaur ★★

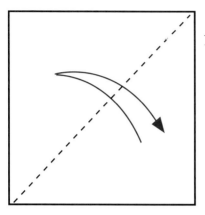

1. First fold a piece of paper into a triangle - make a crease and unfold.

2. Now fold the edges to the center crease.

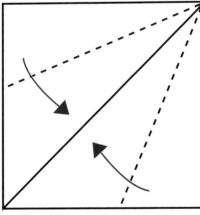

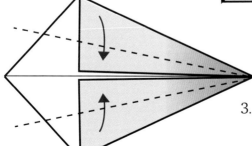

3. Once more fold the edges to the center.

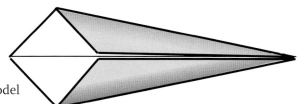

4. This is how your model should look.

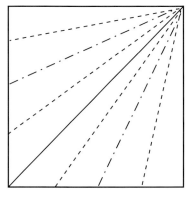

5. Unfold the paper completely, and fold again creating valley folds and mountain folds as in the diagram. Refer to page 6 if unsure about the direction of folds.

- - - - - - - - **Valley Fold**

— · — · — · · **Mountain Fold**

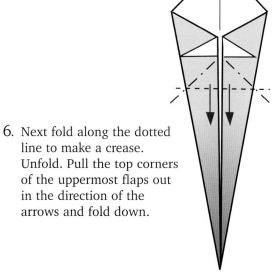

6. Next fold along the dotted line to make a crease. Unfold. Pull the top corners of the uppermost flaps out in the direction of the arrows and fold down.

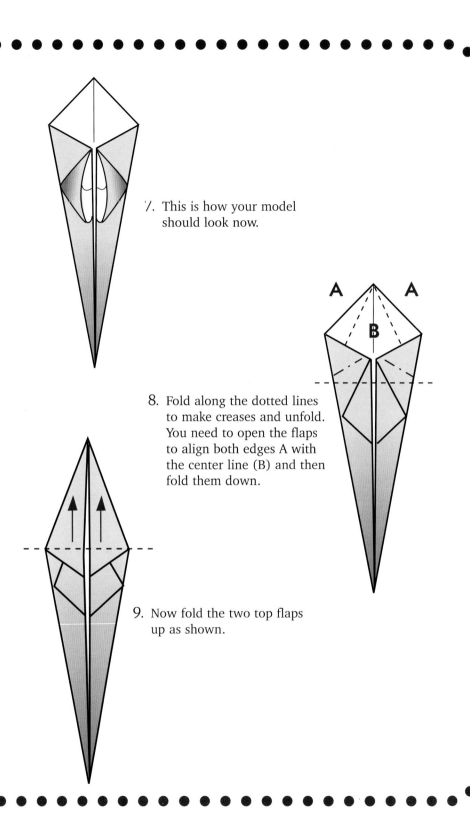

7. This is how your model should look now.

A   A

B

8. Fold along the dotted lines to make creases and unfold. You need to open the flaps to align both edges A with the center line (B) and then fold them down.

9. Now fold the two top flaps up as shown.

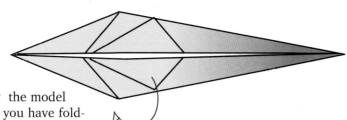

10. This is how the model looks, after you have folded the flaps. Now fold in half away from you.

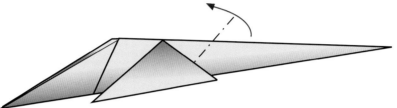

11. Bring the neck up at the line from between the folds by making an Inside Fold.

12. Now fold the corners diagonally along the dotted lines, shown on the diagram. Do the same on the reverse side.

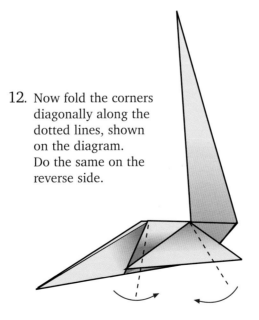

13. Fold down from between the folds to make a beak - by making an Inside Fold.

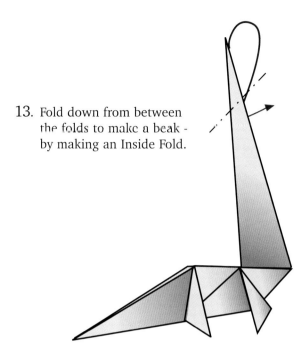

14. Fold the head along the dotted line by making a Staircase Fold.

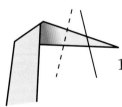

15. Fold the tip along the dotted line.

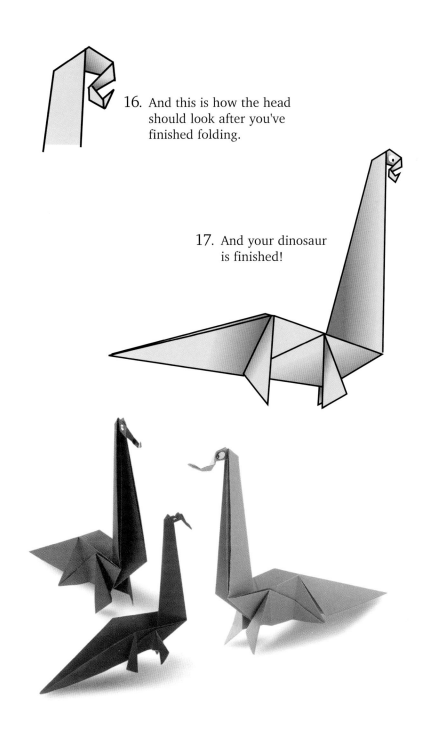

16. And this is how the head should look after you've finished folding.

17. And your dinosaur is finished!

Springy Snake ⭐

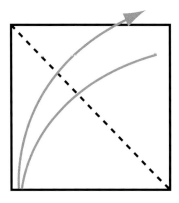

1. Crease paper by folding into a triangle, and then unfold.

2. Repeat to form a triangle in the opposite direction, and then unfold.

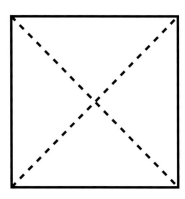

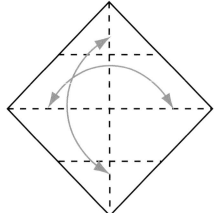

3. Place paper on an angle so that a corner is at the top. Fold the outer corners to the middle of the paper. Then fold outside edges along the dotted lines towards the center.

4. Fold outside edges towards the center along the dotted lines.

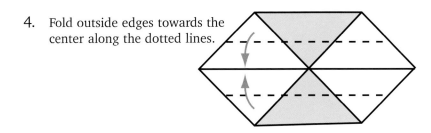

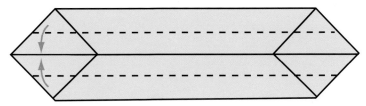

5. Do the same again.

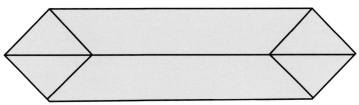

6. Fold the model in half towards you.

7. Fold the end of the strip towards you along the dotted line. This forms the snake's neck.

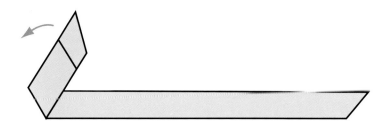

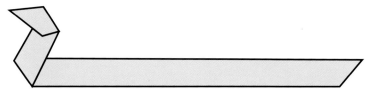

8. Make a fold along the dotted line, to form Samantha's head.

9. Fold the body of the snake towards you, then away from you, along the dotted lines to complete your snake.

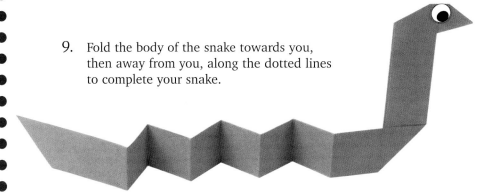

Toad ★★

To create the toad you'll need a square piece of paper no smaller than 3.5 x 3.5 inches (9cm by 9cm). Begin with the colored side of the paper facing you.

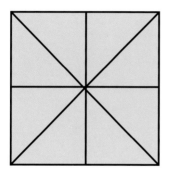

1. Crease paper along the dotted lines. First, crease paper in half towards you. Then crease paper into a triangle on each side.

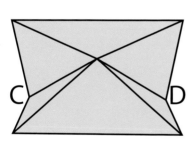

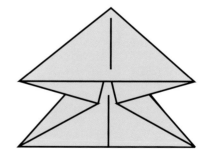

2. Push inwards on points C and D while folding the top and bottom edges of the paper together. This makes a triangle with the base facing you.

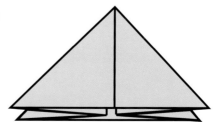

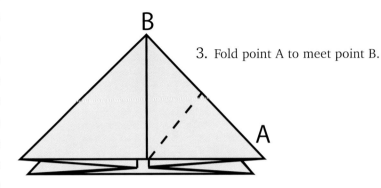

3. Fold point A to meet point B.

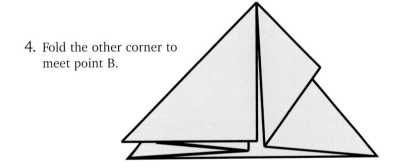

4. Fold the other corner to meet point B.

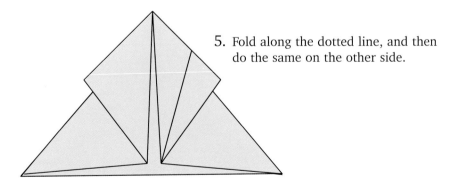

5. Fold along the dotted line, and then do the same on the other side.

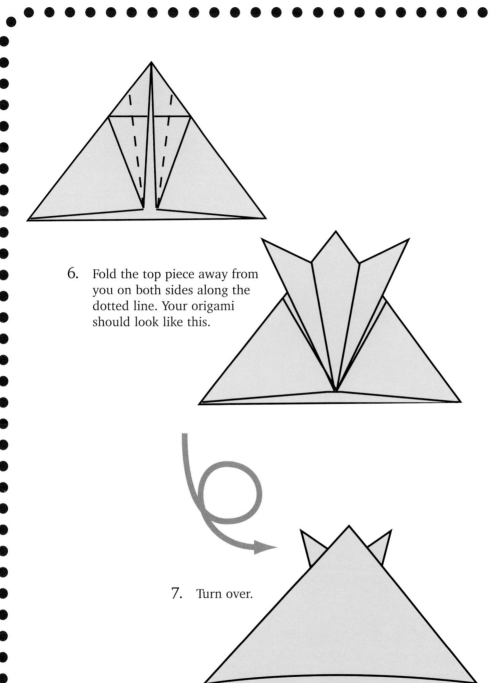

6. Fold the top piece away from you on both sides along the dotted line. Your origami should look like this.

7. Turn over.

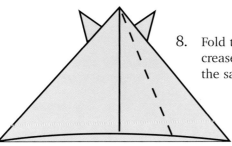

8. Fold towards you along the crease on the right side. Do the same on the left side.

9. Fold away from you along the dotted lines so your origami looks like ths. Turn over.

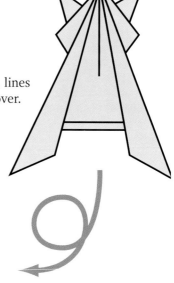

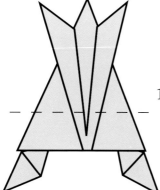

10. Fold the top triangular piece in half along the dotted line, folding away from you.

11. Then fold along the dotted line back toward you.

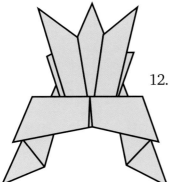

12. Your origami should look like the picture here.

13. Turn over, and your toad is ready to jump!

14. If you like, you can draw some eyes on his face.

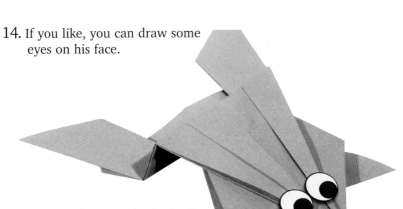

You can push down on the back of your toad, where the two top folds meet, to make him jump.

Piranha ★★

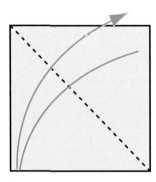 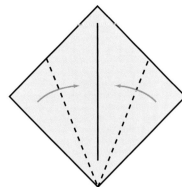

1. Crease paper in half so that it forms a triangle, then unfold.

2. Fold both side edges along the dotted lines to the center crease.

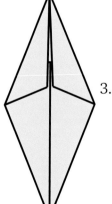

3. Fold the two upper edges to the center crease along the dotted lines. This is called a diamond base.

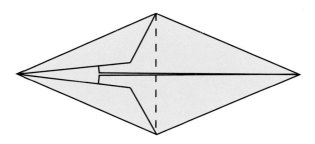

4. Fold in half along the dotted line to form a crease, then back. You should now have a diamond base with a crease across the middle.

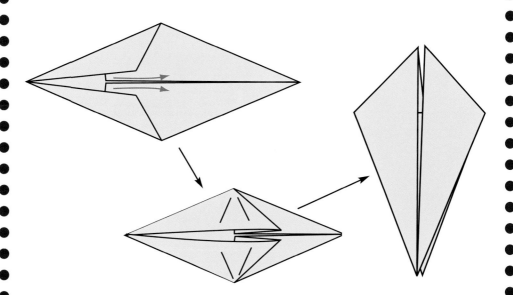

5. Grab the two corners of the paper that are hidden behind the top flaps. Pull these corners out, then flatten and tuck under so that your model looks like the picture above.

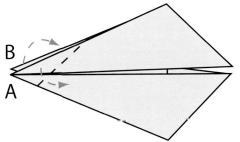

6. Fold your model in half by folding the right side behind the left side.

7. Fold the top flap down towards you. Then fold the bottom flap upwards to form the piranha's tail.

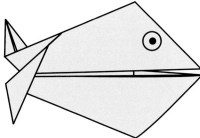

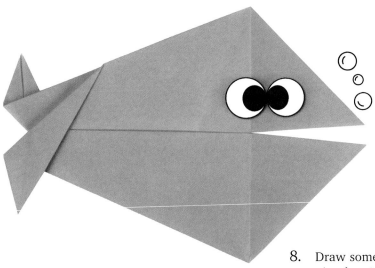

8. Draw some eyes on your piranha. Grab each flap of his tail and pull them in opposite directions to make him prey on anything in sight!

Bat ★★

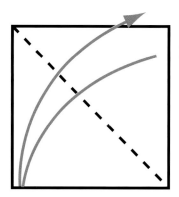

1. Crease paper by folding it into a triangle. Then unfold.

2. Fold paper in half the other way, then unfold.

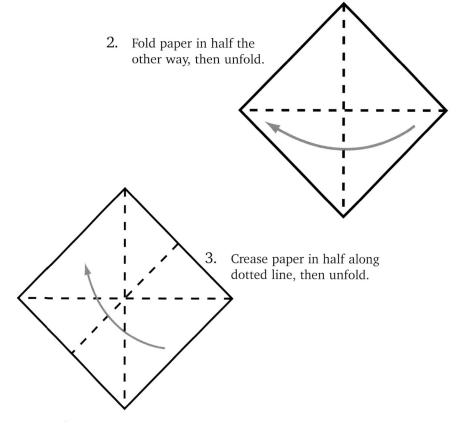

3. Crease paper in half along dotted line, then unfold.

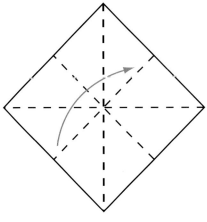

4. Crease paper along dotted line once again.

5. Squash outside edges together along the center crease and fold them down towards the base edge to form a triangle.

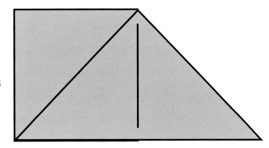

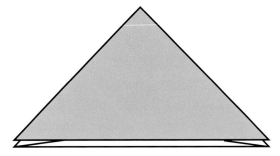

6. Fold the top point of the triangle down to the opposite edge.

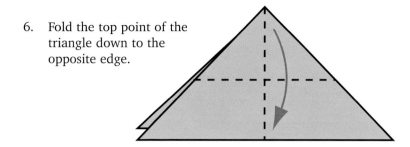

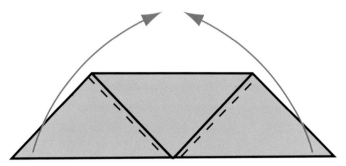

7. Fold the top flaps upwards along the dotted lines.

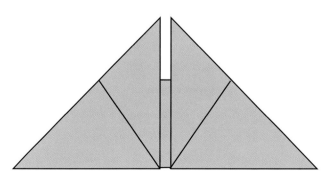

Your origami should now look like the above picture.

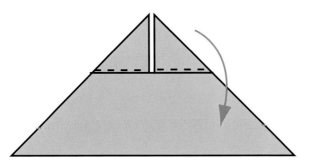

8. Turn over. Fold the two top triangle sections downwards along the dotted line.

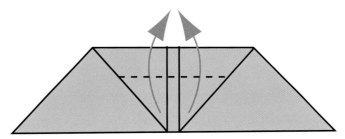

9. Fold the bottom points in the direction of the arrow so they are overlapping the back fold.

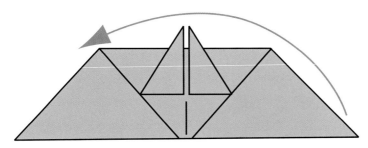

10. Fold the whole model in half, away from you in the direction of the arrow.

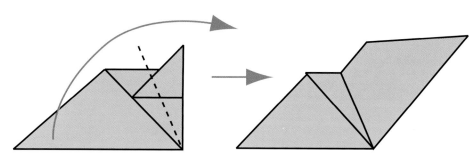

11. Fold inwards along the dotted line and then take the wing at point A and fold out

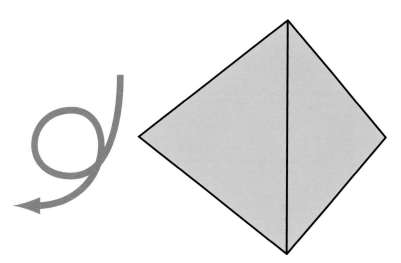

12. Turn over to repeat on the other side. Your origami should look like the picture above.

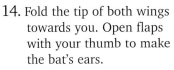

13. Let model spring open as shown. Fold away from you along the dotted lines to form the bat's wings.

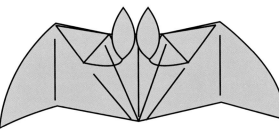

14. Fold the tip of both wings towards you. Open flaps with your thumb to make the bat's ears.

Vulture ★★

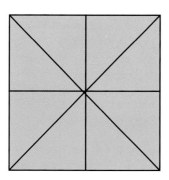

1. Crease paper along the dotted lines. First, crease paper in half towards you. Then crease paper into a triangle on each side.

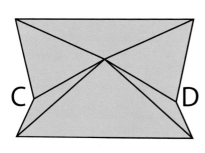

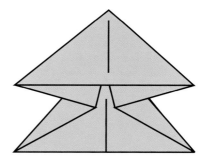

2. Push inwards on points C and D while folding the top and bottom edges of the paper together. This makes a triangle with the base facing you.

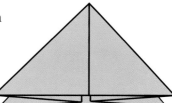

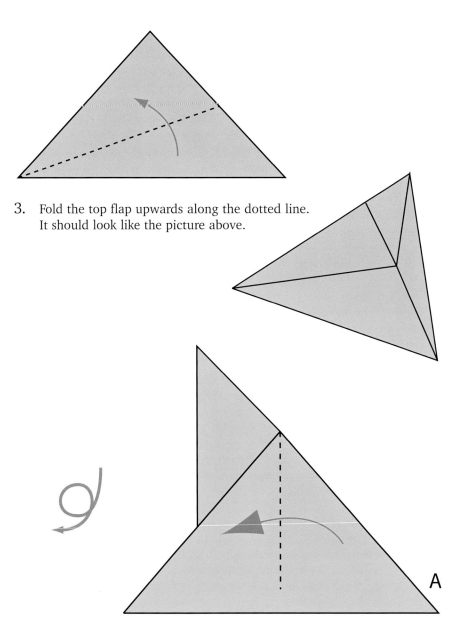

3. Fold the top flap upwards along the dotted line. It should look like the picture above.

4. Turn over. Fold the top flap A towards the left.

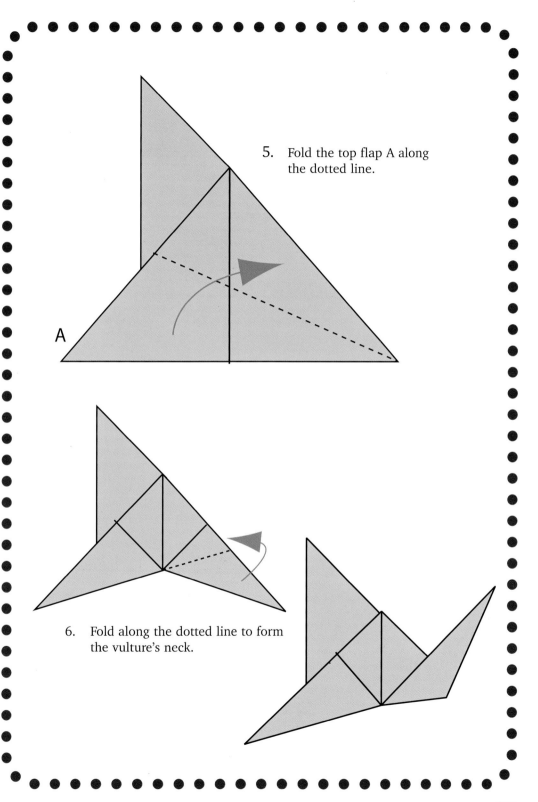

5. Fold the top flap A along the dotted line.

A

6. Fold along the dotted line to form the vulture's neck.

7. Fold the tip towards you to form the vulture's head.

Exotic Flowers

The charm of the origami lily lies in its ability to remind us of the real thing. You could make several in different colors and arrange them in a vase.

The flower ball looks wonderful when six flowers are joined together, but try tying a cotton thread to a single flower and hanging it in your window, or on the Christmas tree.

Lily ★★★

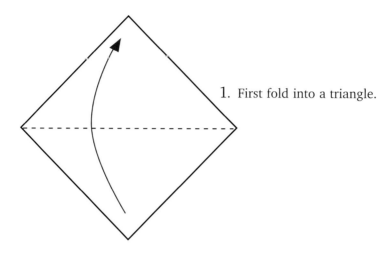

1. First fold into a triangle.

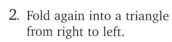

2. Fold again into a triangle from right to left.

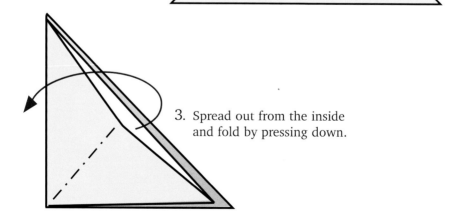

3. Spread out from the inside and fold by pressing down.

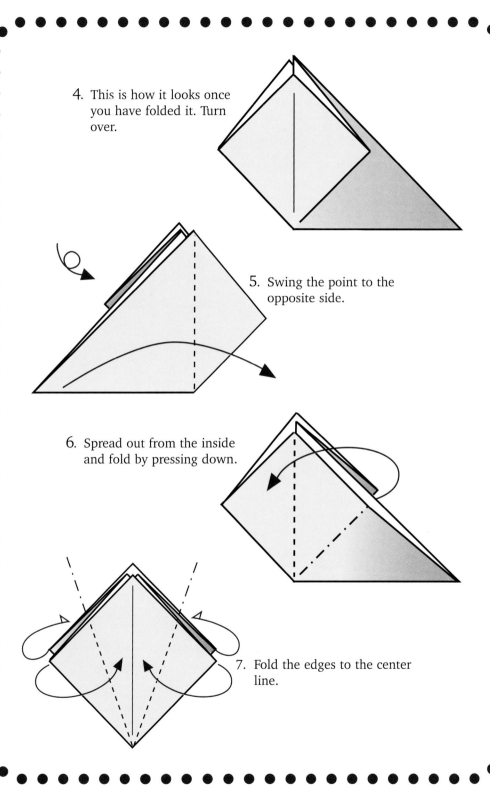

4. This is how it looks once you have folded it. Turn over.

5. Swing the point to the opposite side.

6. Spread out from the inside and fold by pressing down.

7. Fold the edges to the center line.

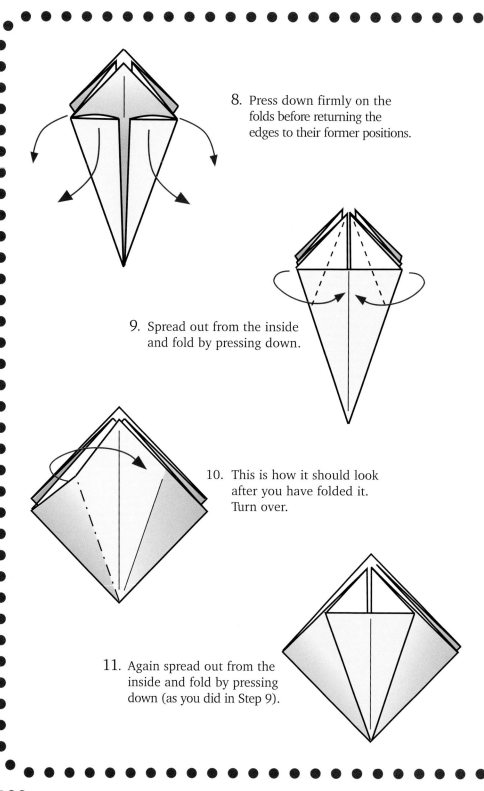

8. Press down firmly on the folds before returning the edges to their former positions.

9. Spread out from the inside and fold by pressing down.

10. This is how it should look after you have folded it. Turn over.

11. Again spread out from the inside and fold by pressing down (as you did in Step 9).

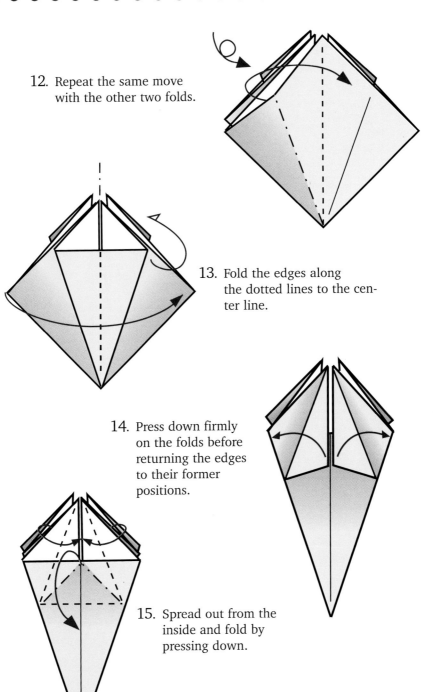

12. Repeat the same move
with the other two folds.

13. Fold the edges along
the dotted lines to the center line.

14. Press down firmly
on the folds before
returning the edges
to their former
positions.

15. Spread out from the
inside and fold by
pressing down.

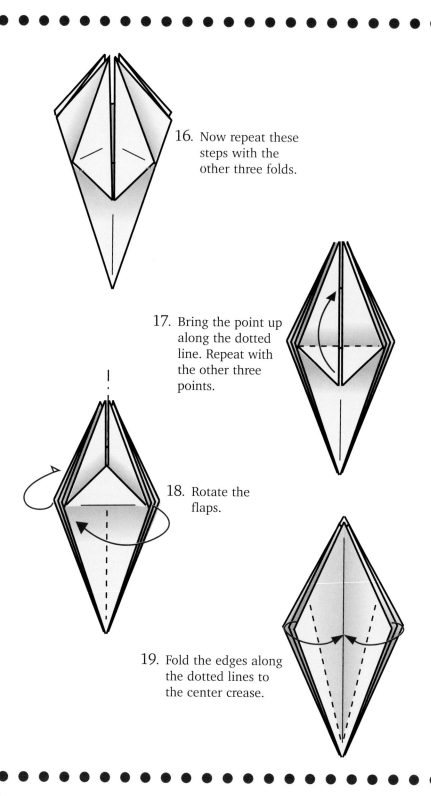

16. Now repeat these steps with the other three folds.

17. Bring the point up along the dotted line. Repeat with the other three points.

18. Rotate the flaps.

19. Fold the edges along the dotted lines to the center crease.

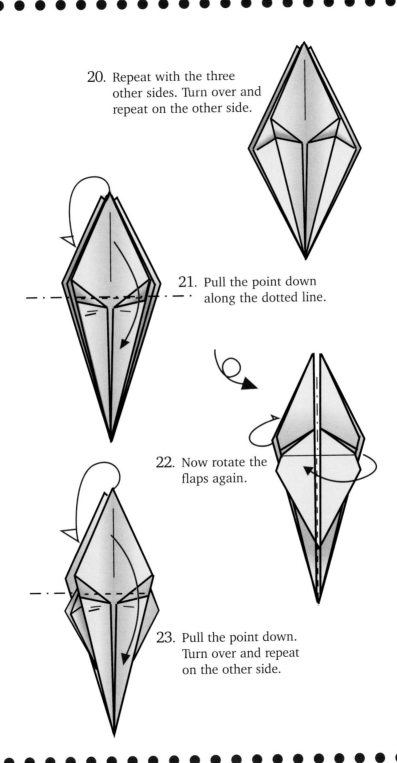

20. Repeat with the three other sides. Turn over and repeat on the other side.

21. Pull the point down along the dotted line.

22. Now rotate the flaps again.

23. Pull the point down. Turn over and repeat on the other side.

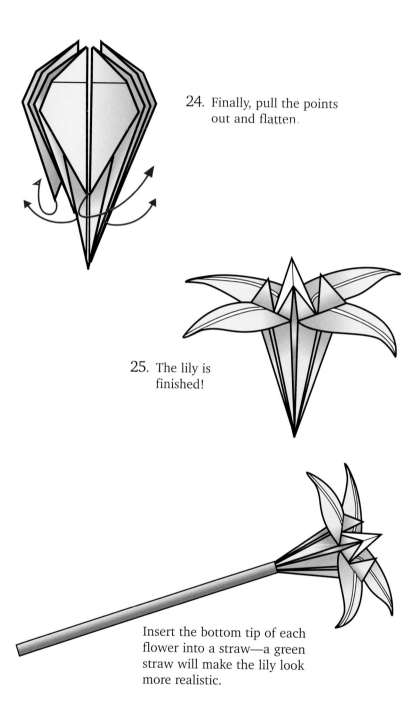

24. Finally, pull the points out and flatten.

25. The lily is finished!

Insert the bottom tip of each flower into a straw—a green straw will make the lily look more realistic.

Flower Ball ★★★

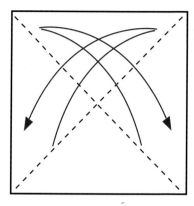

1. Fold the paper into a triangle to make creases both ways. Unfold.

2. Now fold into a rectangle both ways again to make creases. Turn over.

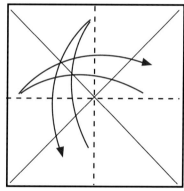

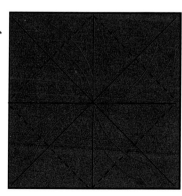

3. Fold all four corners to the center to make creases. Turn over again.

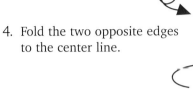

4. Fold the two opposite edges to the center line.

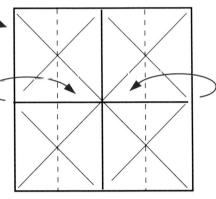

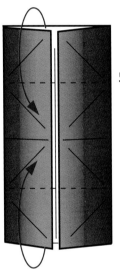

5. Fold the upper and lower edges to the center.

6. Using the arrows as a guide, pull the corners out and fold down.

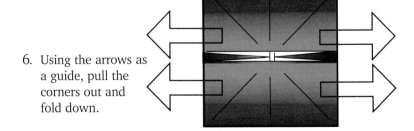

7. This is what the model looks like now. Continue to pull out each corner and fold down.

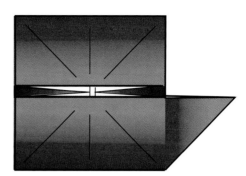

8. Spread out from the inside and fold by pressing down.

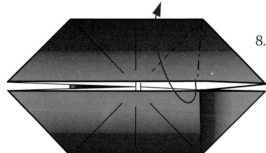

9. This is how it should look after you have folded one. Do the same for all flaps.

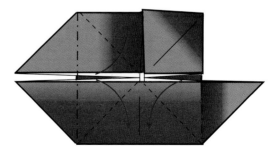

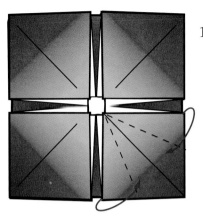

10. Fold the edges to the center crease.

11. Spread out from the inside and fold by pressing down.

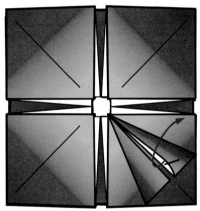

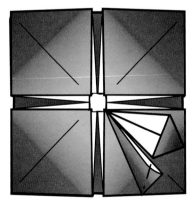

12. Do the same with the other flap.

13. This is how it looks after folding two flaps. Fold all the other flaps now.

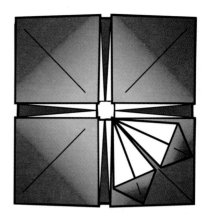

14. Fold all four corners to the back. This is what the model looks like after you've finished folding the corners back.

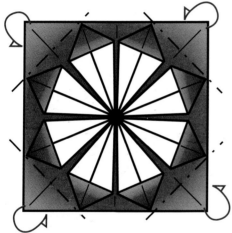

15. By attaching a ribbon to the edge of a flower, you have made a pretty decoration.

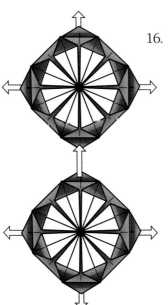

16. Or, if you'd like to continue, pull back the folded corner flaps. Make six flowers like the first one and put them together by pasting the corner flaps to form a flower ball.

17. You can use it by itself as a decoration, or hang it in a window by attaching a fine cotton string or thin ribbon.

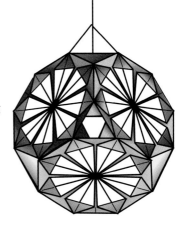

Index